ARE YOU READY?

ARE YOU READY?

DR. CHANDRAKUMAR MANICKAM

CREATION HOUSE
A STRANG COMPANY

Are You Ready? by Chandrakumar Manickam
Published by Creation House
A Strang Company
600 Rinehart Road
Lake Mary, Florida 32746
www.creationhouse.com

Unless otherwise noted, all Scripture quotations are from the New American Standard Bible Updated Edition, Copyright © 1960, 1962, 1963, 1968, 1971, 1972, 1973, 1975, 1977, 1995 by The Lockman Foundation. Used by permission. (www. Lockman.org)

Scripture quotations marked NIV are from the Holy Bible, New International Version of the Bible. Copyright © 1973, 1978, 1984, International Bible Society. Used by permission.

Design Director: Bill Johnson
Cover design by Amanda Potter

Library of Congress Control Number: 2008937221
International Standard Book Number: 978-1-59979-522-5

First Edition

08 09 10 11 12 — 987654321
Printed in the United States of America

CONTENTS

1 What Is Eschatology?.................................. 1

2 Why Study Eschatology?........................... 5

3 The Coming of Christ and the Rapture.................. 9

4 Events in Heaven After the Rapture...................... 53

To Contact the Author 73

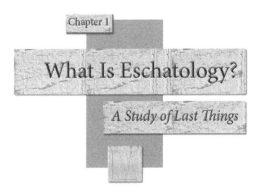

Chapter 1

What Is Eschatology?

A Study of Last Things

ESCHATOLOGY IS A study of last things. It is a branch of theology that deals with the doctrine of the events of the last days. It is also the study of the final events, the second coming of Christ, or the "last times," as spoken of in the Bible. (See Matthew 24:3–31.)

Eschatology, properly understood, embraces the far-reaching prophecy concerning the Lord Jesus Christ as Prophet, Priest, and King, and as the promised Seed.

It embraces prophecy concerning the church, involving the translation of the living saints, the judgment seat of Christ, the Marriage Supper of the Lamb, and the return of the glorified church to reign with Christ. It brings to picture the eternal state of the messianic kingdom.

A STUDY OF BIBLICAL PROPHESIES

The study of prophecy or God's revealed plan for the last days has become more relevant with the increasing tensions in the Middle Eastern countries and between the powerful Western nations. The possibility of a nuclear holocaust threatens the existence of humankind.

Terrorism is on the increase, and the world leaders tremble with fear at the immense problems among the nations. But Bible-believing Christians know that God is in control of the nations, and He will end the world according to His predetermined plan. (See Matthew 24:42–44.)

Several prophecies made by God through His prophets have been fulfilled in the past, and this gives us the confidence that the remaining prophecies will also come to pass.

Piecing together the who, what, when, where, and why's of Bible prophecy and its fulfillment is like putting the pieces of a puzzle together while looking through a dark glass. But the pieces are on the board, and a true picture is evolving out of it.

A Study of Events

There are many events that take place in the eschatological understanding: the return of Christ (1 Thess. 4:15–16); the dead raised and the living transformed (1 Cor. 15:51–52); Christ's rule (Rev. 11:15); angry nations; God's wrath; the dead judged; rewards given; and sinners destroyed (Rev. 11:18). Eschatology was at the center of apostolic teaching and Christ Himself taught the imminent end of the age.

Biblical eschatology is thus concerned not only with the destiny of the individual but also with history. God does not only reveal Himself by means of inspired men, but also in and through the events of redemptive history, the most important of which are the advent and the life of Jesus Christ.

2

As we read Matthew 24, all the events are given in detail in the words of Christ Himself. Eschatology is not merely a legend or an obscure story, but the Scriptural accounts tell of a real thing that is going to happen. As Christians, what are we supposed to do? Does the Bible tell us to sit quietly and wait upon the return of our Lord? Or does it remind us to warn others, too, so that people will be aware of what is going to happen?

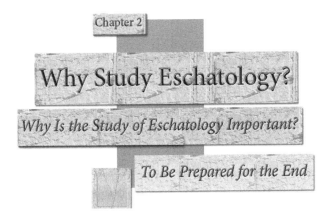

Chapter 2

Why Study Eschatology?

Why Is the Study of Eschatology Important?

To Be Prepared for the End

Anyone would desire to know the ultimate outline of eternity, what lies beyond the grave, and therefore, it is important to study eschatology. Very often preachers speak to their congregations about what will come to pass at the end of the age, but most of them do not adequately teach on this subject. Therefore, the study of this particular subject is necessary. It will help the believers to be aware and to be ready to face the things that will come to pass very soon.

The Word of God urges us to know about the hope of things to come. God is telling us to be diligent in presenting ourselves approved as workers who do not need to be ashamed, handling accurately the Word of God (2 Tim. 2:15).

IT PROVIDES SPIRITUAL COMFORT

The knowledge of prophecy is spiritually stimulating. It induces a Christian to lead a life pleasing to God. Christianity could not have survived without this prophecy of living hope, the hope of our resurrection to eternal life.

The study of eschatology fulfills our mental urge to know more. It answers our questions about our future destiny. It never leaves us in uncertainty. Rather, it gives a better picture of the events that are yet to pass.

The study of eschatology well ahead of the End Times will stabilize our emotional balances in times of tribulation in so much as the knowledge of prophecy gives comfort to the suffering.

> For if we believe that Jesus died and rose again, even so God will bring with Him those who have fallen asleep in Jesus. For this we say to you by the word of the Lord, that we who are alive and remain until the coming of the Lord, will not precede those who have fallen asleep.
>
> —1 Thessalonians 4:14–15

It Builds Up Faith and Hope

> For the Lord Himself will descend from heaven with a shout, with the voice of the archangel and with the trumpet of God, and the dead in Christ will rise first. Then we who are alive and remain will be caught up together with them in the clouds to meet the Lord in the air, and thus we shall always be with the Lord. Therefore comfort one another with theses words.
>
> —1 Thessalonians 4:16–18

The recognition of Christ's return gives us an urge not only to live a holy life but also to serve Him diligently.

The knowledge of the end-time events gives us a new standard of evaluation regarding the best usage of our time. The Bible is the only book that gives authoritative information about the future.

> For truly I [Jesus] say to you, until heaven and earth pass away, not the smallest letter or stroke shall pass away from the Law until all is accomplished.
>
> —MATTHEW 5:18

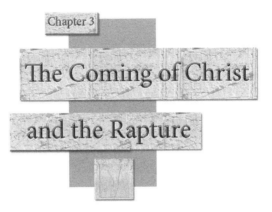

Chapter 3

The Coming of Christ and the Rapture

THE GREEK TERM that refers to the rapture is found in 1 Thessalonians 4:17, where it is translated as "caught up." This phrase is used in the New American Standard Version, the King James Version, and New International Version of the Bible.

From this translation, we understand that at the coming of the Christ in the end, the faithful will be raptured and taken up by Christ.

We shall see in order the events that are to take place during the rapture of the church—the secret coming of Christ.

SIGNS OF CHRIST'S COMING FOR HIS OWN

What did Jesus say about His Coming?

> And as He was sitting on the Mount of Olives, the disciples came to Him privately, saying, "Tell us, when will these things happen, and what will be the sign of Your coming, and of

the end of the age?" And Jesus answered..."For many will come in My name, saying, 'I am the Christ,' and will mislead many. You will be hearing of wars and rumors of wars. See that you are not frightened, for those things must take place, but that is not yet the end. For nation will rise against nation, and kingdom against kingdom, and in various places there will be famines and earthquakes. But all these things are merely the beginning of birth pangs. Then they will deliver you to tribulation, and will kill you, and you will be hated by all nations because of My name. And at that time many will fall away and will betray one another and hate one another. Many false prophets will arise and will mislead many. Because lawlessness is increased, most people's love will grow cold. But the one who endures to the end, he will be saved. The gospel of the kingdom shall be preached in the whole world as a testimony to all the nations, and then the end will come."

—MATTHEW 24:3–14

For the coming of the Son of Man will be just like the days of Noah. For as in those days before the flood they were eating and drinking, marrying and giving in marriage, until the day that Noah entered the ark, and they did not understand until the flood came and took them all away; so will the coming of the Son of Man be.

—MATTHEW 24:37–39

We have all heard about Noah and the Flood, which destroyed the then-known world because of the people's sinfulness. Only Noah's family was saved because of their righteousness. We see in the Bible that God warned Noah regarding the great destruction of the sinful world. What was that warning? It was regarding the judgment of God.

> Then God said to Noah, "The end of all flesh has come before Me; for the earth is filled with violence because of them; and behold, I am about to destroy them with the earth....Behold, I, even I am bringing the flood of water upon the earth, to destroy all flesh in which is the breath of life, from under heaven; everything that is on the earth shall perish."
>
> —GENESIS 6:13, 17

> Then the LORD said to Noah, "Enter the ark, you and all your household, for you alone I have seen to be righteous before Me in this time."
>
> —GENESIS 7:1

The same warning is given to us who are living in this present world. In the time of Noah it was a warning of destruction through water, but now the warning is that the judgment of God will come upon the ungodly people by way of destruction through fire.

> But by His word the present heavens and earth are being reserved for fire, kept for the day of judgment and destruction of ungodly men.
>
> —2 PETER 3:7

Our world is in a worse state now than it was in the days of Noah, and the judgment of God is going to come very soon upon this earth. Today, everywhere in this world we hear of wars and rumors of wars. All the nations are preparing themselves for a war, one that the Bible talks about. (See Mathew 24:4–8.) It is called the war of Armageddon. This will be a war against Israel. Already, all the Arab countries are fighting against Israel and they are not able to do anything because Israelites are the chosen people of the only true and living God. He is Jesus Christ our Lord.

Soon there is going to be an atomic war that the world has never tasted before. The Bible says that the world at that time was destroyed being flooded with water and the present heavens and Earth are being reserved for fire, kept for the day of judgment and destruction of ungodly men. (See 2 Peter 3:6–7.)

We are living in such a terrible stage of history now. This is what Peter prophesied:

> But the day of the Lord will come like a thief, in which the heavens will pass away with a roar and the elements will be destroyed with intense heat, and the earth and its works will be burned up. Since all these things are to be destroyed in this way, what sort of people ought you to be in holy conduct and godliness, looking for and hastening the coming of the day of God, because of which the heavens will be destroyed by burning, and the elements will melt with intense heat.
>
> —2 PETER 3:10–12

12

AS IN THE DAYS OF NOAH

Just as Jesus predicted, today we witness everything happening just as they happened in the days of Noah. We shall see them one by one as given below.

1) Spiritual decline

Just as there was spiritual decline in the days of Noah, we see today that people are so caught up in the materialistic world and they do not feel the need of looking up to God. Generally, there is no fear of God.

In the days of Noah, people forgot their God and lived a life of materialism and secularism. In fact, faith in God was in danger of extinction altogether, except for eight people—the family of Noah, whom God saved from destruction. The days in which we live are much the same. All the countries of the world are fast becoming pagan. Several affluent and Western nations have become increasingly materialistic, immoral, and depraved.

2) Social dilemma

Just like the society was so corrupted in the days of Noah, even so today the society is highly corrupted and several of the so-called Christian ministries have become commercialized. Ministry has become more of a profession than a commission from God.

In the days of Noah there was a tremendous increase in crime and an enormous gain in world population. Today in our world we see the crime rate rising at an alarming speed. Skyjackings, kidnappings, and wanton murders are increasing. The world population is increasing like a nightmare.

One must only take note of the rising number of

terrorist attacks to see that lawlessness is increasing each day.

> Because lawlessness is increased, most people's love will grow cold.
>
> —MATTHEW 24:12

3) Shameless depravity

Just as in the days of Noah, today people do disgraceful things in public without any shame. Wickedness and immorality captured the people in the days of Noah. Now, erotic books and photos, public nudity, pornographic films, and crowded divorce courts are all manifestations of the sex revolution that is sweeping our world.

4) Scientific development

The days of Noah were the days of advancing language, knowledge, and trade. It is superfluous to discuss the scientific development of our day, but it is significant to mention that Daniel prophesied that at the end of the age there would be an explosion of knowledge. (See Daniel 12:4.) Suffice it to say that today we have new scientific discoveries that allow mankind to do both good and bad quickly.

5) Strong delusion

Just as in the days of Noah, the devil has prevented many people from perceiving the difference between reality and falsehood.

The days of Noah were days of strong delusion. Their eyes were so blinded by materialism that they could not foresee the judgment of God. Matthew 24:39 says, "They did not understand until the flood came and took them all away." Today we see people lost in this materialistic, corrupted world. They have no hope of any future in their current state, but they are not being cautioned about the judgment to come.

You are fortunate to read this book because you can learn about the judgment of God.

6) Many people's love will grow cold

> And because lawlessness is increased, most people's love will grow cold.
>
> —MATTHEW 24:12

In accordance with Jesus' statement that most people's love will grow cold, very often we read in the news about children turning against the parents and the parents turning against their children—even to the extent of killing each other.

A shocking report was given by the BBC in February 2006 that one man from the Mayi-Mayi tribe in Nyonga in the Katanga province of the Congo confessed that he had eaten his wife. The reporter also said he had witnessed tribe members cutting parts off the local chief, beginning with his fingers and his innards. They threw them in the pot with oil and onions and cooked them.

7) Some devotion

Just as in the days of Noah, worldliness has taken over godliness. When God told Noah to build the ark, there were only a few who showed some devotion to God. Noah was a man of God and preached for 120 years, but only eight people obeyed the voice of God and were saved from the Flood. Today we are living in a time with ever-increasing access to preaching. The gospel is being preached to almost all the remote parts of this earth. God is at work setting the stage for the final drama.

8) Many will fall away from the Lord in the Last Days

We are living in very difficult days before the rapture of the church. Before the Antichrist comes to power, there will be a great falling away from the foundations of the Christian faith. We are currently in this time of apostasy, which was predicted in the Bible:

> Let no one in any way deceive you, for it will not come unless the apostasy comes first, and the man of lawlessness is revealed, the son of destruction.
>
> —2 THESSALONIANS 2:3

We are living in those days now! Never before have we seen such apostasy, with no concern by the people involved. There are many who profess to be believers in Christ but instead have rejected the foundations of the Christian faith.

Beware, as we live in dangerous days.

9) False prophets will mislead many

> And Jesus answered and said to them, "See to it that no one misleads you. For many will come in My name, saying, 'I am the Christ,' and will mislead many."
>
> —MATTHEW 24:4–5

The Antichrist is the political ruler who will do the works of Satan. The false prophet will be the religious ruler who will undergird the work of Antichrist. Both will get their power from Satan.

The false prophet will do the work of a prophet in that he will draw the attention of the people toward the Antichrist, saying that he is the Christ and that the nations should worship him. The false prophet will imitate many miracles of God. He might cause fire to come down from heaven, imitating the miracles of Elijah in order to convince the nation of Israel that he is the Elijah, who the Jews are expecting to return. By performing several such miracles, he will try to deceive the people of Israel to believe that the Antichrist is truly the messiah they are waiting for. Several occult practices are creeping into Christian churches already.

The Bible has much to say about false prophets.

> For false Christs and false prophets will arise, and will show signs and wonders, in order to lead astray, if possible, the elect.
> —MARK 13:22

> Then if any one says to you, "Behold, here is the Christ," or "There He is," do not believe him.
> —MATTHEW 24:23

> For such men are false apostles, deceitful workers, disguising themselves as apostles of Christ. And no wonder, for ever Satan disguises himself as an angel of light.
> —2 CORINTHIANS 11:13–14

During this period of time, the false prophet, with

the Antichrist, will launch the great, worldwide religious system and will command tremendous power to work his evil deeds.

10) Sudden destruction

Jesus said to his disciples:

> And just as it happened in the days of Noah, so it shall be also in the days of the Son of Man: they were eating, they were drinking, they were marrying, they were being given in marriage, until the day that Noah entered the ark, and the flood came and destroyed them all. It was the same as happened in the days of Lot: they were eating, they were drinking, they were buying, they were selling, they were planting, they were building; but on the day that Lot went out from Sodom it rained fire and brimstone from heaven and destroyed them all.
>
> —LUKE 17:26–29

> The world at that time was destroyed, being flooded with water. But by His word the present heavens and earth are being reserved for fire, kept for the day of the judgment and destruction of ungodly men.
>
> —2 PETER 3:6–7

> It will be just the same on the day that the Son of Man is revealed.
>
> —LUKE 17:30

The Flood came and swept the people of the world away. Only those who entered Noah's ark were saved.

Today God has provided an ark in Jesus Christ. He is our way of escape. Jesus said, "I am the way, and the truth, and the life; no one comes to the Father but through Me" (John 14:6). Where are you going? Who is leading your life? Whom are you following? What is the aim and hope of your life? Jesus Christ is the only hope.

There are only two alternatives, either the love of God or the wrath of God. Either receive the love of God and be saved from condemnation, or the wrath of God will take you to the burning hellfire.

> For God so loved the world, that He gave His only begotten Son, that whoever believes in Him should not perish, but have eternal life.
> —JOHN 3:16

God, the greatest lover with the greatest degree of love, loved the greatest number of people with the greatest sacrificial love and gave the greatest gift, His only begotten Son. Through Him God gave the greatest invitation—that whosoever believeth in Him, the greatest Person, should not perish. This is the greatest deliverance through which man can have the greatest possession, eternal life.

A rejected opportunity to give is a lost opportunity to receive. Unless you give, you shall not receive. Would you give yourself to the Lord Jesus and receive eternal life? "Behold, I have told you in advance," says the Lord (Matt. 24:25).

You will be hearing of wars.

And you will be hearing of wars and rumors of wars. See that you are not frightened, for those things must take place, but that is not yet the end.

—MATTHEW 24:6

There are wars that divide nations from within and from without. They are not the conventional wars that are fought by some countries today.

The future of the Middle East is very much moving towards a nuclear build-up in Iran that could lead to a huge confrontation between Iran and Israel, bringing to the forefront the confrontation prophesied in Ezekiel 38. In that prophetic scripture, Gog (which could represent Russia) and Persia (possibly a representation of Iran), among others, have a major and catastrophic confrontation with Israel. Russia is already assisting Iran with the nuclear technology it needs to build its own bombs, while at the same time, other countries from the East have assisted Iran in building missiles with nuclear capability and the range to reach Israel.

The growing Russian empire

While violence in the Middle East has been escalating at an unprecedented rate in recent years, that area has never seen such wars and such slaughter as will occur during the last days and during the Tribulation period.

And the instigator of the first great war will be none other than Russia and her allies. However, this war will bring the day that Russia dies.

Nation will rise against nation, kingdom against kingdom.

For nation will rise against nation, and kingdom against kingdom.

—MATTHEW 24:7

Several million soldiers have died in the wars of the twentieth century. The Iraq war and the aftermath of it, which has developed into a civil war, seem to be a never-ending catastrophe.

There will be famines.

In various places there will be famines.

—MATTHEW 24:7

Jesus told us there would be famines in the last days. (See Matthew 24:7.) Famines are reported from different parts of the world. Numerous religious groups and nonprofit organizations are currently seeking to end world hunger in nearly every corner of the globe.

There will be earthquakes.

There will be…earthquakes.

—MATTHEW 24:7

Earthquakes have become a common occurrence in the recent past. In the twentieth century alone, countless people died in earthquakes and through the floods, fires, and famines that resulted from them.

One of the first recorded earthquakes is described in 1 Kings 19:11–12, and one of the most remarkable ones occurred at the time of our Savior's crucifixion (Matt.

27:51). Earthquakes are revealed with the introduction of the seven trumpets in Revelation.

Earthquakes serve to remind us that God is still on the throne. They also reveal man's utter helplessness and should awaken us to our need for the Savior.

> And behold, the veil of the temple was torn in two from top to bottom; and the earth shook and the rocks were split.
>
> —MATTHEW 27:51

You will be hated on account of My name.

> Then they will deliver you to tribulation, and will kill you, and you will be hated by all nations because of My name.
>
> —MATTHEW 24:9

> Know this first of all, that in the last days mockers will come with their mocking, following after their own lusts, and saying, "Where is the promise of His coming? For ever since the fathers fell asleep, all continues just as it was from the beginning of creation.
>
> —2 PETER 3:3–4

11) Persecution

When our Lord Jesus was pleased to take upon Himself the form of a servant and go about preaching the kingdom of God, He took all opportunities to forewarn His disciples of the many distresses, afflictions, and persecutions they should expect to endure for His name's sake. The apostle Paul, following the steps of our Lord, takes particular care to warn young Timothy of the difficulties he could expect to meet over the course of his ministry. Today, more Christians are being martyred than in any other period in history.

Though all believers will face persecutions, their trials may come in differing degrees. All Christians will find by their own experience that whether they act in a private or public capacity, they must in some degree or other suffer persecution. Not all who are persecuted are real Christians, for many sometimes suffer and are persecuted for having done wrong rather than for righteousness' sake. The most important question is, Are you still faithful to God in spite of being persecuted for godly living?

Why should we expect persecution?

We may be assured to expect persecution for a number of reasons.

First, because our Lord taught in Matthew 5:10, "Blessed are those who are persecuted for the sake of righteousness, for theirs is the kingdom of heaven."

Secondly, our Lord Himself experienced it. Follow the Lord from the manger to the cross and see if you (or anyone else you have ever known or heard of) have gone through any persecution like that which the Son of God endured while He was on the planet Earth. He was hated by wicked men, reviled, counted and called a blasphemer, a drunkard, a Samaritan, and a devil; He was stoned, thrust out of the synagogues, called a deceiver of people. As an enemy of Caesar, He was scourged, spit upon, condemned, and nailed to an accursed tree.

Thirdly, the saints of all ages experienced persecution and are experiencing it now. We see how Abel was made a martyr for his religion and how the son of the bondwoman mocked Isaac. As we read the Acts of the Apostles, we see how the early Christians were threatened, stoned, imprisoned, scourged, and martyred. Even today many saints in the communist lands are undergoing severe persecutions.

Fourthly, persecution comes from the sinner's enmity against God. Wicked men hate God and therefore cannot but hate those who are godly.

Fifthly, the godly need persecution. Why should the godly go through suffering and persecution? Apostle Paul, in his letter to the Corinthians, lifts the veil of his private life and allows us to catch a glimpse of his private life and of his human frailties and needs. He very clearly records the specifics of his anguish, tears, affliction, and satanic opposition. He provides details of his persecution, loneliness, imprisonments, beatings, feelings of despair, hunger, shipwrecks, sleepless nights, and that "thorn in the flesh"—his companion of pain. It makes us feel close to him as we picture him as a man with real, down-to-Earth problems just like you and me have.

Paul gives three reasons for our suffering and persecution in 2 Corinthians 1:3–11:

- "That we will be able to comfort those who are in any affliction" (v. 4)—God allows suffering so that we might have the capacity to enter into the sorrows and afflictions of others. If you have suffered the loss of your husband, your wife, or your child, you may share in complete sympathy with someone else with a similar kind of a loss. Our loss and tragedies allow us to have a better understanding of their situation.

- "That we would not trust in ourselves" (v. 9)—God also allows suffering and persecution in our lives so that we might learn what it means to depend on Him, not on our own strength and resources. Again and again He reminds us of the consequences of pride, but sometimes we only learn the lesson through suffering.

- "That thanks may be given" (v. 11)—God trains us to give thanks in everything. Sometimes one of the reasons why our suffering is prolonged is that we take so long to say, "Thank you, Lord, for this suffering or this experience."

What have we endured for the Lord?

Suffering for Christ's sake should be viewed as a privilege. Let us learn to pray:

Lord, help me to see the sunshine through the
   rain,
What I count loss may somehow be gain.
Help me to sing when I would cry,
Knowing that thou art standing by.
What matters if this life is brief?
What matters if I've toil or grief?
I, in my Savior, find relief.
Of all my joy, He is the chief.
God reigns! I will be true.

We need to be faithful in our private life, public life, penny life, priestly calling, and in persecution. Let us totally pour out our lives at the altar and be faithful servants of God.

> If you were of the world, the world would love its own; but because you are not of the world, but I chose you out of the world, because of this the world hates you...If they persecuted Me, they will also persecute you...because they do not know the One who sent Me.
>
> —JOHN 15:19–21

> An hour is coming for everyone who kills you to think that he is offering service to God. These things they will do because they have not known the Father or Me.
>
> —JOHN 16:2–3

> Brother will betray brother to death, and a father his child; and children will rise up against parents and have them put to death. And you will be hated by all because of My name, but the one who endures to the end, he will be saved.
>
> —MARK 13:12–13

> The whole world lies in the power of the evil one.
>
> —1 JOHN 5:19

Then they will deliver you to tribulation, and will kill you, and you will be hated by all nations because of My name.

—MATTHEW 24:9

And you will even be brought before governors and kings for My sake, as a testimony to them and to the Gentiles. But when they hand you over, do not worry about how or what you are to say; for it shall be given you in that hour what you are to say. For it is not you who speak, but it is the Spirit of your Father who speaks in you. Brother will betray brother to death, and a father his child; and children will rise up against parents and cause them to be put to death. And you will be hated by all because of My name, but it is the one who has endured to the end who will be saved.

—MATTHEW 10:18–22

But thanks be to God, who always leads us in His triumph in Christ, and manifests through us the sweet aroma of the knowledge of Him in every place. For we are a fragrance of Christ to God among those who are being saved and among those who are perishing; to the one an aroma from death to death, to the other an aroma from life to life. And who is adequate for these things?

—2 CORINTHIANS 2:14–16

But I do not consider my life of any account as dear to myself, in order that I may finish my course, and the ministry which I received from the Lord Jesus, to testify solemnly of the gospel of the grace of God.

—ACTS 20:24

But we have this treasure in earthen vessels, that the surpassing greatness of the power will be of God and not from ourselves; we are afflicted in every way, but not crushed; perplexed, but not despairing; persecuted, but not forsaken; struck down, but not destroyed; always carrying about in the body the dying of Jesus, so that the life of Jesus also may be manifested in our body.

—2 CORINTHIANS 4:7–10

"So I will choose their punishments, And I will bring on them what they dread. Because I called, but no one answered; I spoke, but they did not listen. And they did evil in My sight And chose that in which I did not delight." Hear the word of the LORD, you who tremble at His word: "Your brothers who hate you, who exclude you for My name's sake, Have said, 'Let the LORD be glorified, that we may see your joy.' But they will be put to shame."

—ISAIAH 66:4–5

Blessed are you when men hate you, and ostracize you, and insult you, and scorn your name as evil, for the sake of the Son of Man. Be glad in that day and leap for joy, for behold, your reward is great in heaven; for in the same way their fathers used to treat the prophets.

—LUKE 6:22–23

Do you suppose that I came to grant peace on earth? I tell you, no, but rather division; for from now on five members in one household will be divided, three against two and two against three. They will be divided, father against son and son against father, mother against daughter and daughter against mother, mother-in-law against daughter-in-law and daughter-in-law against mother-in-law.

—LUKE 12:51–53

So that on the contrary you should rather forgive and comfort him, otherwise such a one might be overwhelmed by excessive sorrow. Wherefore I urge you to reaffirm your love for him. For to this end also I wrote, so that might put you to the test, whether you are obedient in all things. But whom you forgive anything, I forgive also; for indeed what I have forgiven, if I have forgiven anything, I did it for your sakes in the presence of Christ.

—2 CORINTHIANS 2:7–10

Be of sober sprit, be on the alert. Your adversary, the devil, prowls about like a roaring lion, seeking someone to devour. But resist him, firm in your faith, knowing that the same experiences of suffering are being accomplished by your brethren who are in the world. After you have suffered for a little while, the God of all grace, who called you to His eternal glory in Christ, will Himself perfect, confirm, strengthen, and establish you. To Him be dominion forever and ever. Amen.

—1 PETER 5:8–11

And upon her forehead a name was written, a mystery, "BABYLON THE GREAT, THE MOTHER OF HARLOTS AND OF THE ABOMINATIONS OF THE EARTH." And I saw the woman drunk with the blood of the saints, and with the blood of the witnesses of Jesus. And when I saw her, I wondered greatly. And the angel said to me, "Why do you wonder? I will tell you the mystery of the woman and of the beast that carries her, which has the seven heads and the ten horns. The beast that you saw was, and is not, and is about to come up out of the abyss and go to destruction. And those who dwell on the earth, whose name has not been written in the book of life from the foundation of the world, will wonder when they see the beast, that he was and is not and will come."

—REVELATION 17:5–8

And the dragon stood on the sand of the seashore. Then I saw a beast coming up out of the sea, having ten horns and seven heads, and on his horns were ten diadems, and on his heads were blasphemous names. And the beast which I saw was like a leopard, and his feet were like those of a bear, and his mouth like the mouth of a lion. And the dragon gave him his power and his throne and great authority. And I saw one of his heads as if it had been slain, and his fatal wound was healed. And the whole earth was amazed and followed after the beast; they worshiped the dragon because he gave his authority to the beast; and they worshiped the beast, saying, "Who is like the beast, and who is able to wage war with him?" There was given to him a mouth speaking arrogant words and blasphemies, and authority to act for forty-two months was given to him. And he opened his mouth in blasphemies against God, to blaspheme His name and His tabernacle, that is, those who dwell in heaven. It was also given to him to make war with the saints and to overcome them, and authority over every tribe and people and tongue and nation was given to him. And all who dwell on the earth will worship him, everyone whose name has not been written from the foundation of the world in the book of life of the Lamb who has been slain.

—REVELATION 13:1–8

After this I saw four angels standing at the four corners of the earth, holding back the four winds of the earth, so that no wind should blow on the earth or on the sea or on any tree. And I saw another angel ascending from the rising of the sun, having the seal of living God; and he cried out with a loud voice to the four angels to whom it was granted to harm the earth and the sea, saying, "Do not harm the earth or the sea or the trees until we have sealed the bond-servants of our God on their foreheads." And I heard the number of those who were sealed, one hundred and forty-four thousand sealed from every tribe of the sons of Israel.

—REVELATION 7:1–4

To prepare His people for future events, Jesus told His disciples:

Now learn the parable from the fig tree: when its branch has already become tender and puts forth its leaves, you know that summer is near; So, you too, when you see all these things, recognize that He is near, right at the door.

—MATTHEW 24:32–33

Therefore be on alert, for you do not know which day your Lord is coming.

—MATTHEW 24:42

THE END SHALL COME WHEN THE GOSPEL REACHES THE WHOLE WORLD

The gospel has almost reached the whole world and the end is about to come soon. There has been an explosive growth of Christianity in Asia and Africa, and the flame of revival can be seen in America. Oceania, too, has seen a growth of several Spirit-filled churches in the past ten years. Only the Antarctic and the mainland of Europe have yet to experience a great revival, and I believe the momentum is building up. Several of the current world events draw us closer to the Rapture of the church.

Many things mentioned in the Bible are already occurring in the world in greater intensity than they have ever occurred before. In the days of Noah, wickedness was great in the earth. In these last days, as we are very close to the coming of Christ, we are witnessing terrible wickedness, and in every walk of life we see evil men and women occupying sensitive and strategic positions of power in major cities of the world.

The Bible says, "But evil men and impostors will proceed from bad to worse, deceiving and being deceived" (2 Tim. 3:13).

In the days of Noah, the world was unaware of approaching disaster. It is true of events in the last days, according to what Jesus said.

> Be on guard, that your hearts may not be weighted down with dissipation and drunkenness and the worries of life, and that day will not come on you suddenly like a trap; for it will come upon all those who dwell on the face of all the earth.
>
> —Luke 21:34–35

Just as Noah and his family entered the ark at the appointed time, the Word promises the following:

> The Lord Himself will descend from heaven
> with a shout, with the voice of the archangel,
> and with the trumpet of God, and the dead in
> Christ will rise first. Then we who are alive and
> remain will be caught up together with them
> in the clouds to meet the Lord in the air, and
> so we shall always be with the Lord.
>
> —1 Thessalonians 4:16–17

We are witnessing the signs of His coming in these last days, and while there have always been wars, rumors of wars, famines, pestilences, earthquakes, and wickedness, it is important to note that all these signs have never ever been present simultaneously with such intensity during the same period of time.

That's why these words spoken by Jesus are so significant for our day and age:

> But when these things begin to take place,
> straighten up and lift up your heads, because
> your redemption is drawing near.
>
> —Luke 21:28

God's Timetable

When will it take place?

The salt, the believers in Christ, of our society would be removed at the time of the Rapture.

> But of that day and hour no one knows, not
> even the angels of heaven, nor the Son, but
> the Father alone. For the coming of the Son
> of Man will be just like the days of Noah. For

as in those days before the flood they were eating and drinking, marrying and giving in marriage, until the day that Noah entered the ark, and they did not understand until the flood came and took them all away, so will the coming of the Son of Man be. Then there will be two men in the field; one will be taken and one will be left. Two women will be grinding at the mill; one will be taken and one will be left. Therefore be on the alert, for you do not know which day your Lord is coming.

—MATTHEW 24:36–42

Paul says very clearly that it will take place before the Antichrist is revealed.

Then that lawless one will be revealed whom the Lord will slay with the breath of His mouth and bring to an end by the appearance of His coming.

—2 THESSALONIANS 2:8

For this reason you also must be ready; for the Son of Man is coming at an hour when you do not think He will.

—MATTHEW 24:44

How will it take place?—The manner of His Coming

And after He had said these things, He was lifted up while they were looking on, and a cloud received Him out of their sight. And as they were gazing intently into the sky while He was going, behold, two men in white clothing stood beside them. They also said, "Men of Galilee, why do you stand looking into the sky? This Jesus, who has been taken up from you into heaven, will come in just the same way as you have watched Him go into heaven.

—ACTS 1:9–11

Every eye will see Him.

The Bible makes it very clear that when the Lord appears on the clouds at the time of Rapture, literally every single person—the dead and the living—will see Him.

BEHOLD, HE IS COMING WITH THE CLOUDS, and every eye will see Him, even those who pierced Him; and all the tribes of the earth will mourn over Him. So it is to be. Amen.

—REVELATION 1:7

The believers in Christ shall hear the voice of the Son of God.

Truly, truly, I say to you, an hour is coming and now is, when the dead will hear the voice of the Son of God, and those who hear will live....Do not marvel at this; for an hour is coming, in which all who are in the tombs will hear His voice, and will come forth; those who did the good deeds to a resurrection of life, those who committed the evil deeds to a resurrection of judgment.

—JOHN 5:25, 28–29

People without Christ shall not hear the voice of the Son of God.

> They answered Him, "We are Abraham's descendents and have never yet been enslaved to anyone; how is it that You say, 'You will become free'?"
>
> —JOHN 8:33

> He who is of God hears the words of God; for this reason you do not hear them, because you are not of God.
>
> —JOHN 8:47

> But we do not want you to be uninformed, brethren, about those who are asleep, that you will not grieve as do the rest who have no hope. For if we believe that Jesus died and rose again, even so God will bring with Him those who have fallen asleep in Jesus. For this we say to you by the word of the Lord, that we who are alive and remain until the coming of the Lord, will not precede those who have fallen asleep. For the Lord Himself will descend from heaven with a shout, with the voice of the archangel and with the trumpet of God, and the dead in Christ will rise first. Then we who are alive and remain will be caught up together with them in the clouds to meet the Lord in the air, and so we will always be with the Lord. Therefore comfort one another with these words.
>
> —1 THESSALONIANS 4:13–18

The First Resurrection

The Fact of Christ's Resurrection

Now I make known to you, brethren, the gospel which I preached to you, which also you received, in which also you stand, by which also you are saved, if you hold fast the word which I preached to you, unless you believed in vain. For I delivered to you as of first importance what I also received, that Christ died for our sins according to the Scriptures, and that He was buried, and that He was raised on the third day according to the Scriptures, and that He appeared to Cephas, then to the twelve. After that he appeared to more than five hundred brethren at one time, most of whom remain until now, but some have fallen asleep; then he appeared to James, then to all the apostles; and last of all, as to one untimely born, He appeared to me also. For I am the least of the apostles, and not fit to be called an apostle, because I persecuted the church of God. But by the grace of God I am what I am, and His grace toward me did not prove vain; but I labored even more than all of them, yet not I, but the grace of God with me. Whether then it was I or they, so we preach and so you believed. Now if Christ is preached, that He has been raised from the dead, how do some among you say that there is no resurrection of the dead? But if there is no resurrection of the dead, not even Christ has been raised; and if

Christ has not been raised, then our preaching is vain, your faith also is vain. Moreover we are even found to be false witnesses of God, because we testified against God that He raised Christ, whom He did not raise, if in fact the dead are not raised. For if the dead are not raised, not even Christ has been raised; and if Christ has not been raised, your faith is worthless; you are still in your sins. Then those also who have fallen asleep in Christ have perished. If we have hoped in Christ in this life only, we are of all men most to be pitied.

—1 CORINTHIANS 15:1–19

The Order of Resurrection

But now Christ has been raised from the dead, the first fruits of those who are asleep. For since by a man came death, by a man also came the resurrection of the dead." "For as in Adam all die, so also in Christ all shall be made alive. But each in his own order: Christ the first fruits, after that those who are Christ's at his coming, then comes the end, when He delivers up the kingdom to the God and Father, when He abolished all rule and all authority and power." "For He must reign until He has put all His enemies under His feet. The last enemy that will be abolished is death "For he has put all things in subjection under his feet. But when He says, 'All things are put in subjection,' it is evident that He expected who put all things in subjection to Him. And when all things are subjected to Him, then the Son Himself also will be subjected to the One who subjected all things to Him, that God may be all in all. Otherwise, what will those do who are baptized for the dead? If the dead are raised at all, why then are they baptized for them?" "Why are we also in danger every hour? I protest, brethren, by the boasting in you, which I have in Christ Jesus our Lord, I die daily. If from human motives I fought with wild beasts at Ephesus, what does it profit me? If the dead are not raised, let us eat and drink, for tomorrow we die."

—1 CORINTHIANS 15:20–32

The Mystery of Resurrection

Now I say this, brethren, that flesh and blood cannot inherit the kingdom of God; nor does the perishable inherit the imperishable. Behold, I tell you a mystery; we will not all sleep, but we will all be changed, in a moment, in the twinkling of an eye, at the last trumpet; for the trumpet will sound, and the dead will be raised imperishable, and we will be changed. For this perishable must put on the imperishable, and this mortal must put on immortality. But when this perishable will have put on the imperishable, and this mortal will have put on immortality, then will come about the saying that is written, "DEATH IS SWALLOWED UP in victory. O DEATH, WHERE IS YOUR VICTORY? O DEATH, WHERE IS YOUR

STING?" The sting of death is sin, and the power of sin is the law; but thanks be to God, who gives us the victory through our Lord Jesus Christ. Therefore, my beloved brethren, be steadfast, immovable, always abounding in the work of the Lord, knowing that your toil is not in vain in the Lord.

—1 CORINTHIANS 15:50–58

For our citizenship is in heaven, from which also we eagerly wait for a Savior, the Lord Jesus Christ; who will transform the body of our humble state into conformity with the body of His glory, by the exertion of the power that He has even to subject all things to Himself.

—PHILIPPIANS 3:20–21

We also read in 1 Thessalonians 4:16–18, "For the Lord Himself will descend from heaven with a shout, with the voice of the archangel and with the trumpet of God; and the dead in Christ will rise first. Then we who are alive and remain will be caught up together with them in the clouds, and so we shall always be with the Lord. Therefore comfort one another with these words."

When the Rapture does occur, billions of people will be left behind full of surprise and shock at the disappearances of their loved ones, friends, and acquaintances.

Beloved, now we are children of God, and it has not appeared as yet what we will be. We know that when He appears, we will be like Him, because we will see Him Just as He is.

—1 JOHN 3:2

For you have died and your life is hidden with Christ in God. When Christ, who is our life, is revealed, then you also will be revealed with Him in glory.

—COLOSSIANS 3:3–4

Jesus said to her, "I am the resurrection and life; he who believes in Me will live even if he dies, and everyone who lives and believes in Me will never die. Do you believe this?"

—JOHN 11:25–26

Now, little children, abide in Him, so that when He appears, we may have confidence and not shrink away from Him in shame at His coming.

—1 JOHN 2:28

Blessed and holy is the one who has a part in the first resurrection; over these the second death has no power, but they will be priests of God and of Christ and will reign with Him for a thousand years.

—REVELATION 20:6

THE TRANSFORMATION THE BODIES OF BELIEVERS

Do not be deceived: "Bad company corrupts good morals." Become sober-minded as you ought, and stop sinning; for some have no knowledge of God. I speak this to your shame. But someone will say, "How are the dead raised?

And with what kind of body do they come?" You fool! That which you sow does not come to life unless it dies; and that which you sow, you do not sow the body which is to be, but a bare grain, perhaps of wheat or of something else. But God gives it a body just as He wished, and to each of the seeds a body of its own. All flesh is not the same flesh, but there is one flesh of men, and another flesh of beasts, and another flesh of birds, and another of fish. There are also heavenly bodies and earthly bodies, but the glory of the heavenly is one, and the glory of the earthly is another. There is one glory of the sun, and another glory of the moon, and another glory of the stars; for star differs from star in glory. So also is the resurrection of the dead. It is sown a perishable body, it is raised an imperishable body; it is sown in dishonor, it is raised in glory; it is sown in weakness, it is raised in power; it is sown a natural body, it is raised a spiritual body. If there is a natural body, there is also a spiritual body. So also it is written, "The first MAN, Adam, BECAME A LIVING SOUL." The last Adam became a life-giving spirit. However, the spiritual is not first, but the natural; then the spiritual. The first man is from the earth, earthy; the second man is from heaven. As is the earthy, so also are those who are earthy; and as is the heavenly, so also are those who are heavenly. And just as we have borne the image of the earthy, we shall also bear the image of the heavenly.

—1 CORINTHIANS 15:33–49

The Rapture of the Church

How to be prepared to meet the Lord

You need to be spiritually clean, eagerly receptive, and genuinely desiring in order to meet the Lord. Your expectancy of His return will help you to be ready.

> For you yourselves know full well that the day of the Lord will come just like a thief in the night. While they are saying, "Peace and safety!" then destruction will come upon them suddenly like birth pangs upon a woman with child, and they will not escape. But you, brethren, are not in darkness, that the day would overtake you like a thief; for you are all sons of light and sons of day. We are not of night or of darkness; so then let us not sleep as others do, but let us be alert and sober.
> —1 Thessalonians 5:2–6

To understand the deeper truth about Christ's second coming, it is essential that we are rightly dividing the Word of truth about it. His return has two phases or two separate time-events. The first phase is *Rapture*, at which time Jesus will come for His saints, and the second phase is *revelation*, at which time Jesus will come with His saints.

The Rapture takes place in the air; the revelation occurs on the earth. The Rapture is being caught up with the Lord; the revelation is being revealed by the Lord. The Rapture brings bliss to the people of God; the revelation brings judgment to the nations and their citizens who have rejected God.

At the time of Rapture, the coming of the Lord will be like that of a thief in the night. This implies that it is secretive and unnoticed. At the time of revelation, by contrast, it shall be public and every eye shall see Jesus returning.

> BEHOLD, HE IS COMING WITH THE CLOUDS, and every eye will see Him, even those who pierced Him; and all the tribes of the earth will mourn over Him. So it is to be. Amen.
>
> —REVELATION 1:7

The word *rapture* itself does not appear in the Bible, but the concept is clearly there. We read in the Bible: "For the Lord Himself will descend from heaven with a shout, with the voice of the archangel and with the trumpet of God; and the dead in Christ will rise first. Then we who are alive and remain shall be caught up together with them in the clouds to meet the Lord in the air, and so we shall always be with the Lord" (1 Thess. 4:16–17).

"Caught up" is the English equivalent of *harpazo* in the Greek language of the New Testament. When this term was translated into Latin for Roman readers, the word used was *rapia*, and this is the root word for our English word for *rapture*. So, in an indirect way, the word *rapture* is in the Bible.

> Take heed, keep on the alert; for you do not know when the appointed time will come. It is like a man away on a journey, who upon leaving his house and putting his slaves in charge, assigning to each one his task, also

commanded the doorkeeper to stay on the
alert. Therefore, be on the alert—for you do not
know when the master of the house is coming,
whether in the evening, at midnight, or when
the rooster crows, or in the morning—in case
he should come suddenly and find you asleep.
—MARK 13:33–36

Jesus' coming will be immensely significant—for both
believers and unbelievers.

For the coming of the Son of Man will be just
like the days of Noah. For as in those days
which were before flood they were eating and
drinking, marrying and giving in marriage,
until the day that Noah entered the ark, and
they did not understand until the flood came
and took them all away, so shall the coming of
the Son of Man be. Then there will be two men
in the field; one will be taken and one will be
left. Two women will be grinding at the mill;
one will be taken and one will be left.
—MATTHEW 24:37–41

When the great Flood occurred, only the people inside
the ark with Noah escaped the devastation. When the
Rapture occurs, only the born-again people of God will
be taken into custody with the Lord. From this time
onward, the raptured believers in Christ will start a new
relationship with Christ in the symbolism of marriage.
The church is the bride and Jesus is the Bridegroom. (See
2 Corinthians 11:2.) The next event will be the Marriage
Supper of the Lamb. (See Revelation 19:7–9.)

THE RAPTURE AND THE SECOND COMING ARE TWO DIFFERENT EVENTS

The Rapture and the second coming of Christ are two distinct and different events. The Rapture is when Jesus comes on the clouds for the believers in the Christ. The Second Coming is when Jesus comes back to Earth and His feet will stand on the Mount of Olives.

Rapture	Second Coming
Jesus will come to receive the believers in Christ. "Do not let your heart be troubled; believe in God, believe also in Me. In My Father's house are many dwelling places; if it were not so, I would have told you; for I go to prepare a place for you. If I go and prepare a place for you, I will come again and receive you to Myself, that where I am, there you may be also" (John 14:1–3). "For if we believe that Jesus died and rose again, even so God will bring with Him those who have fallen asleep in Jesus. For this we say to you by the word of the Lord, that we who are alive and remain until the coming of the Lord, will not precede those who have fallen asleep" (1 Thess. 4:14–15).	Jesus will come with the saints of God. "When Christ, who is our life, is revealed, then you also will be revealed with Him in glory" (Col 3:4). (See Zechariah 14:5; Jude 14–15; Revelation 19:14.)
Believers will be caught up with Him on the clouds. (See 1 Thessalonians 4:13–18.)	Jesus' feet will touch the earth. (See Zechariah 14:4; Revelation 19:11–21.)
Believers in Christ will be taken first, unbelievers are left behind. (See 1 Thessalonians 4:16–17.)	The wicked will be removed first, but the righteous (Tribulation saints) will be left behind. (See Matthew 13:28–30.)
Purpose: to present the church to Himself and to the Father (See 2 Corinthians 11:2; Revelation 19:7–9.)	Purpose: to execute judgment on Earth and set up His kingdom (See Jude 14–15; Revelation 19:11–21; Zechariah 14:3–4.)
Marriage: The marriage of Lamb will be in heaven after the Rapture.	War: Marriage will be followed by war on Earth at the Second Coming.

Rapture	Second Coming
It will happen in a moment, in the twinkling of an eye (too fast for eyes to see). (See 1 Corinthians 15:52.)	It will be a slow coming. People will see Him come back. (See Zechariah 12:10; Matthew 24:30; and Revelation 1:7.)
Believers (alive and dead in Christ) will see Him and also hear the sound of trumpet and the voice of the Son of God. (See John 5:25–28; 1 John 3:2; 1 Corinthians 15:52.)	The wicked will see Him but not hear the sound of the trumpet. (See Revelation 1:7.)
Jesus will descend with a shout for resurrection. (See 1 Thessalonians 4:16.)	No shout is mentioned. (See Revelation 19:11–21.)
A resurrection will take place. (See 1 Thessalonians 4:13–18; 1 Corinthians 15:51–54.)	No resurrection is mentioned. (See Revelation 1:7; 19:11–21; Zechariah 12:10; and 14:4–5.)
It could happen at any time. (See Revelation 3:3; 1 Thessalonians 5:4–6.)	Will occur at the end of seven years of tribulation. (See Daniel 9:24–27.)
Angels will be sent to gather the believers.	Angels will be sent forth to gather unbelievers together for judgment. (See Matthew 13:39, 41, 49; 24:31; 25:31; and 2 Thessalonians 1:7–10.)
The dead in Christ and those who are alive will receive imperishable bodies and will return with Jesus to the heavenly abode. (See John 14:2; 1 Thessalonians 4:14–16.)	Believers will return with Jesus to the earth in already resurrected bodies. (See Revelation 19:11–21.)
Jesus does not come on a white horse.	Jesus will return on a white horse. (See Revelation 19:11.)
It is for the believers only (those in Christ). (See 1 Thessalonians 4:14–17.)	It is for the redeemed of Israel and Gentiles. (See Romans 11:25–27; Matthew 25:31–46.)
It brings a message of hope and comfort. (See 1 Thessalonians 4:18; Titus 2:13; 1 John 3:3.)	It is a message of judgment. (See Joel 3:12–16; Revelation 19:11–21.)

His first coming was over 2,000 years ago, when He came on Earth to save man from sin. The Second Coming is an event starting at the Rapture. It contains four phases:

- First, at the Rapture Christ takes the believers out of this world to be with him. (See 1 Thessalonians 4.)

- Second, Christ pours out His judgments on the world during the seven-year Tribulation period.

- Third, at the end of the seven-year Tribulation Christ destroys the Antichrist and his wicked followers. (See Revelation 19.)

- Fourth, Christ sets up his millennial kingdom, prophesied so often in the Old Testament.

The prophetic literature of the Bible forecasts several specific events. The fulfillment of many of these ancient biblical forecasts are recorded and exist as absolute guarantees that what the Bible forecasts for our future will also be accurately fulfilled.

This multitude of prophecy that has been fulfilled or is in the process of being so is beyond coincidence. Its magnitude and its tremendous scope demand an all-powerful superintendence. The Bible reveals God as the motivating force and creative power behind everything in the world.

The truth presented in the Bible is very important

because what is presented in the Bible is not the opinion of philosophers or scientists, but it is God Almighty's message to man in man's language.

> For no prophecy was ever made by an act of human will, but men moved by the Holy Sprit spoke from God.
>
> —2 PETER 1:21

> For prophecy never had its origin in the will of man, but men spoke from God as they were carried along by the Holy Spirit.
>
> —2 PETER 1:21, NIV

Every prophecy about His first coming has been literally fulfilled in time. That is the proof that all the prophecies about His second coming and kingdom will also be fulfilled in the course of time.

The Old Testament prophecy, including Christ's prophecy in Matthew 24, speaks of how the world will come to an end. (The books of Daniel and Revelation in particular set forth that truth very clearly.) The Bible is the only religious book in the world that speaks correctly about both the origin and the end of the world. These days, Bible-believing Christians as well as skeptics are eager to know what the Bible says about the end of the age.

> For just as the lightning comes from the east and flashes even to the west, so shall the coming of the Son of Man be.
>
> —MATTHEW 24:27

In that passage, Jesus is describing the end of the age to His disciples. That end will not be a single, climatic event but a chain of events, all of which are the inevitable consequences of forces that have been at work in society throughout the whole course of history.

Chapter 4

Events in Heaven After the Rapture

FATHER'S HOUSE IN HEAVEN

In My Father's house are many dwelling places; if it were not so, I would have told you; for I go to prepare a place for you. If I go and prepare a place for you, I will come again and receive you to Myself, that where I am, there you may be also.

—JOHN 14:2–3

THE CHURCH IS THE BRIDE OF CHRIST

And I saw the holy city, new Jerusalem, coming down out of heaven from God, made ready as a bride adorned for her husband.

—REVELATION 21:2

Then one of the seven angels who had the seven bowls full of the seven last plagues came and spoke with me, saying, "Come here, I will show you the bride, the wife of the Lamb."

And he carried me away in the Spirit to a great and high mountain, and showed me the holy city, Jerusalem, coming down out of heaven from God.

—REVELATION 21:9–10

Husbands, love your wives, just as Christ also loved the church and gave Himself up for her,

—EPHESIANS 5:25

FOR THIS REASON A MAN SHALL LEAVE HIS FATHER AND MOTHER AND SHALL BE JOINED TO HIS WIFE, AND THE TWO SHALL BECOME ONE FLESH. This mystery is great; but I am speaking with reference to Christ and the church.

—EPHESIANS 5:31–32

For I am jealous for you with a godly jealousy; for I betrothed you to one husband, so that to Christ I might present you as a pure virgin.

—2 CORINTHIANS 11:2

Then Samson went down to Timnah and saw a woman in Timnah, [one] of the daughters of the Philistines. So he came back and told his father and mother, "I saw a woman in Timnah, [one] of the daughters of the Philistines; now therefore, get her for me as a wife." Then his father and his mother said to him, "Is there no woman among the daughters of your relatives, or among all our people, that you go to take a wife from the uncircumcised Philistines?" But

Samson said to his father, "Get her for me, for she looks good to me." However, his father and mother did not know that it was of the LORD, for He was seeking an occasion against the Philistines. Now at that time the Philistines were ruling over Israel. Then Samson went down to Timnah with his father and mother, and came as far as the vineyards of Timnah; and behold, a young lion [came] roaring toward him. The Spirit of the LORD came upon him mightily, so that he tore him as one tears a young goat though he had nothing in his hand; but he did not tell his father or mother what he had done. So he went down and talked to the woman; and she looked good to Samson. When he returned later to take her, he turned aside to look at the carcass of the lion; and behold, a swarm of bees and honey were in the body of the lion. So he scraped the honey into his hands and went on, eating as he went. When he came to his father and mother, he gave [some] to them and they ate [it;] but he did not tell them that he had scraped the honey out of the body of the lion. Then his father went down to the woman; and Samson made a feast there, for the young men customarily did this. When they saw him, they brought thirty companions to be with him. Then Samson said to them, "Let me now propound a riddle to you; if you will indeed tell it to me within the seven days of the feast, and find it out, then I will give you thirty linen wraps and thirty changes of clothes. But if you are unable to tell me, then you shall give me thirty linen wraps and thirty changes of clothes." And they said to him, "Propound your riddle, that we may hear it." So he said to them, "Out of the eater came something to eat, And out of the strong came something sweet." But they could not tell the riddle in three days. Then it came about on the fourth day that they said to Samson's wife, "Entice your husband, so that he will tell us the riddle, or we will burn you and your father's house with fire. Have you invited us to impoverish us? Is this not [so?]" Samson's wife wept before him and said, "You only hate me, and you do not love me; you have propounded a riddle to the sons of my people, and have not told [it] to me." And he said to her, "Behold, I have not told [it] to my father or mother; so should I tell you?" However she wept before him seven days while their feast lasted. And on the seventh day he told her because she pressed him so hard. She then told the riddle to the sons of her people. So the men of the city said to him on the seventh day before the sun went down, "What is sweeter than honey? And what is stronger than a lion?" And he said to them, "If you had not plowed with my heifer, You would not have found out my riddle."

—JUDGES 14:1–18

Laban gathered all the men of the place and made a feast. Now in the evening he took his daughter Leah, and brought her to him; and

[Jacob] went in to her. Laban also gave his maid Zilpah to his daughter Leah as a maid. So it came about in the morning that, behold, it was Leah! And he said to Laban, "What is this you have done to me? Was it not for Rachel that I served with you? Why then have you deceived me?" But Laban said, "It is not the practice in our place to marry off the younger before the firstborn." Complete the week of this one, and we will give you the other also for the service which you shall serve with me for another seven years." Jacob did so and completed her week, and he gave him his daughter Rachel as his wife.

—Genesis 29:22–28

Then the kingdom of heaven will be comparable to ten virgins, who took their lamps and went out to meet the bridegroom. Five of them were foolish, and five were prudent. For when the foolish took their lamps, they took no oil with them, but the prudent took oil in flasks along with their lamps. Now while the bridegroom was delaying, they all got drowsy and began to sleep. But at midnight there was a shout, "Behold, the bridegroom! Come out to meet him." Then all those virgins rose and trimmed their lamps. But the prudent answered, "No, there will not be enough for us and you too; go instead to the dealers and buy some for yourselves." And while they were going away to make the purchase, the bridegroom came, and those who were ready went in with him to the wedding feast; and the door was shut. Later the other virgins also came, saying, "Lord, lord, open up for us." But he answered, "Truly I say to you, I do not know you." Be on the alert then, for you do not know the day nor the hour.

—MATTHEW 25:1–13

At the end of the Tribulation, people who are in heaven (that is, the bride, or the church) will come down out of heaven because they have been there for seven years.

Be like men who are waiting for their master when he returns from the wedding feast, so that they may immediately open the door to him when he comes and knocks.

—LUKE 12:36

After these things I heard something like a loud voice of a great multitude in heaven, saying, "Hallelujah! Salvation and glory and power belong to our God.

—REVELATION 19:1

Let us rejoice and be glad and give the glory to Him, for the marriage of the Lamb has come and His bride has made herself ready. It was given to her to clothe herself in fine linen, bright and clean; for the fine linen is the righteous acts of the saints. Then he said to me, "Write, 'Blessed are those who are invited to the marriage supper of the Lamb.'" And he said to me, "These are true words of God."

—REVELATION 19:7–9

And the armies which are in heaven, clothed in fine linen, white and clean, were following Him on white horses.

—Revelation 19:14

And He will send forth His angels with A GREAT TRUMPET and THEY WILL GATHER TOGETHER His elect from the four winds, from one end of the sky to the other.

—Matthew 24:31

It was also about these men that Enoch, in the seventh generation from Adam, prophesied, saying, "Behold, the Lord came with many thousands of His holy ones.

—Jude 1:14

When Christ, who is our life, is revealed, then you also will be revealed with Him in glory.

—Colossians 3:4

For this reason, rejoice, O heavens and you who dwell in them. Woe to the earth and the sea, because the devil has come down to you, having great wrath, knowing that he has only a short time.

—Revelation 12:12

Yes, the bride is in heaven, and she will come down out of heaven at the end of the Tribulation.

MT. ZION AND NEW JERUSALEM

> But you have come to Mount Zion and to the
> city of the living God, the heavenly Jerusalem,
> and to myriads of angels.
>
> —HEBREWS 12:22

> I have put My words in your mouth and have
> covered you with the shadow of My hand, to
> establish the heavens, to found the earth, and
> to say to Zion, "You are My people."
>
> —ISAIAH 51:16

THE JUDGMENT SEAT OF CHRIST

The term "judgment seat" comes from the Greek word
bema, which refers to the seat of the judge who has to
decide what prize to be given, to whom, and for what
achievement. It is not the judgment seat of the one who
decides punishment for any offender.

> Each man's work will become evident; for the
> day will show it because it is to be revealed
> with fire, and the fire itself will test the quality
> of each man's work.
>
> —1 CORINTHIANS 3:13

> For we must all appear before the judgment seat
> of Christ, so that each one may be recompensed
> for his deeds in the body, according to what he
> has done, whether good or bad.
>
> —2 CORINTHIANS 5:10

If we have hoped in Christ in this life only, we are of all men most to be pitied.

—1 Corinthians 15:19

And you will be blessed, since they do not have the means to repay you; for you will be repaid at the resurrection of the righteous.

—Luke 14:14

Therefore there is now no condemnation for those who are in Christ Jesus.

—Romans 8:1

Then those who feared the Lord spoke to one another, and the Lord gave attention and heard [it,] and a book of remembrance was written before Him for those who fear the Lord and who esteem His name.

—Malachi 3:16

So that the proof of your faith, being more precious than gold which is perishable, even though tested by fire, may be found to result in praise and glory and honor at the revelation of Jesus Christ;

—1 Peter 1:7

The true church will be raptured at the beginning of the seventieth week (1 Thess. 4:15–17), and the judgment of the church may take place first. In 2 Corinthians 5:10 and Romans 14:10, it is stated that the believers are to be brought for an examination before the Son of God. This is also explained in 1 Corinthians 3:9–15.

This event will take place immediately following the Rapture and translation of the church. It will take place in heaven. Since the Bema Judgment follows the Rapture, the clouds must be the scene of it. John 5:22 states that all judgment has been committed to the Son. This means the right of judgment has been given to the Son by the Father, so Jesus Christ is the one who judges.

THE BASIS FOR BEMA JUDGMENT

It is to be carefully observed that the Bema Judgment is not to determine the question of sin, because only believers will be appearing before the Bema. Our salvation is a free gift of God, so the ones who appear before the Bema are believers whose sin is forgiven. (See Hebrews 10:17.) When the word "appear" in 2 Corinthians 5:10 was translated from the original Greek, might have been better to render it "to be made manifest." The verse would then read, "For it is necessary for all of us to be made manifest."

We shall be judged one by one on individual merit according to our deeds, whether good or bad.

REWARDS IN HEAVEN

First Corinthians 3:14–15 declares that there will be a twofold result from believers' work. Their work has either a positive reward or no reward, in which case it is simply worthless. Paul writes, "Each man's work will become evident; for the day will show it because it is to be revealed with fire, and the fire itself will test the quality of each man's work" (1 Cor. 3:13). First the things done in the flesh will be burned up. Such work will not receive any reward, but will suffer loss. To suffer loss does not mean loss of salvation, but the loss of reward. Paul says, "He himself will be saved, yet so as through fire" (1 Cor. 3:15).

The Bible talks about five heavenly rewards:

1. an imperishable wreath for those who exercise self-control in all things (see 1 Corinthians 9:25);

2. a crown of exultation for those who bring people to Christ (see 1 Thessalonians 2:19);

3. the unfading crown of glory for those who prove to be examples to the flock (see 1 Peter 5:4);

4. a crown of righteousness for those who await the second coming of Christ (see 2 Timothy 4:8);

5. the crown of life for those who love Him and who persevere under trial (see James 1:12).

THE MARRIAGE SUPPER OF THE LAMB

In the Old Testament, Israel is called the wife of God. The church is now the bride of Christ and will become the wife of Christ when wedded to Christ at His second coming.

> Blessed are those who are invited to the marriage supper of the lamb.
> —REVELATION 19:9

Now as Christ's triumph is about to be manifest, when

the harvest has been finished and all the saints have been gathered in, it is time for the marriage of the Lamb to His bride. It could not take place while the false bride, Babylon, with her blasphemous pretensions, remains unjudged.

> For as a young man marries a virgin, So your sons will marry you; And as the bridegroom rejoices over the bride, So your God will rejoice over you.
>
> —ISAIAH 62:5

> I will betroth you to Me forever; Yes, I will betroth you to Me in righteousness and in justice, In lovingkindness and in compassion, And I will betroth you to Me in faithfulness. Then you will know the LORD.
>
> —HOSEA 2:19–20

We are told that Jehovah was the great Husband of God's people, Israel:

> As the bridegroom rejoices over the bride, so your God will rejoice over you.
>
> —ISAIAH 62:5

> For your Maker is your Husband—the LORD Almighty is his name.
>
> —ISAIAH 54:5, NIV

The Marriage Supper of the Lamb speaks to us of the full spiritual union of the church with Jesus and the joy and fidelity which ought to exist between God's people and God's Son.

In Jesus' day there were two ceremonies in a marriage. The first was known as the espousal, which can be compared to our modern engagement period. On that occasion the parents of the man and woman would announce their intentions for the couple to be married, and a waiting period of indefinite length would permit all preparations to be made and their pledge confirmed. The wedding celebration completed the formal union in marriage. The apostle Paul referred to this custom when he wrote, "For I am jealous for you with a godly jealousy; for I betrothed you to one husband, so that to Christ I might present you as a pure virgin" (2 Cor. 11:2).

Surprisingly, the Old Testament contains several illustrations of this divine relationship. One is of the first bride, Eve, whom God made from a rib taken from the side of Adam. Likewise, it was from the wounded side of our Lord that His blood poured forth to give life to the church.

Another bride who illustrated this truth is Rebekah. She heard about Isaac, her prospective groom, from a servant who informed her of the greatness of his master. Rebekah was willing to leave her country and go to Isaac because she loved him, though she had never seen him. The church, like Rebekah, has been procured and is awaiting the marriage day.

First, we will look at the wedding garments.

> It was given to her to clothe herself in fine linen, bright and clean; for the fine linen is the righteous acts of the saints.
> —REVELATION 19:8

Jesus told a parable in Mathew 22 that dramatizes the importance of this wedding garment. In the parable, the king held a wedding banquet for his son, and many guests were invited. Each guest was provided with a special robe as he or she entered. The king arrived to join the festivities, and as he circulated among the guests he encountered one who had no wedding garment. The only reason for such a deficiency would be the visitor's preference for his own apparel. It wasn't adequate, and he was expelled from the banquet. Celebrants at the marriage supper of the Lamb must have Jesus' robe of righteousness.

When we go to that great Marriage Supper and we are rewarded for things we have done for the Lord Jesus Christ, we will cherish the crowns we receive for the honor they will accord Him when we worshipfully place them at His feet. They will be our wedding gift to the Groom.

Presenting the Bride

When you think about a perfect marriage, what qualities do you see? I see, first of all, purity. In Ephesians 5:27 we read that Christ will "present to Himself the church in all her glory, having no spot or wrinkle or any such thing." Miraculously, and beautifully, all our imperfections are exchanged for moral purity.

Marriage brings together two persons and makes them a love-impelled couple. Using human phraseology, the Bridegroom has written a love song to His bride. It is the Song of Solomon in eight stanzas in the Old Testament. The theme of the song is "My beloved is mine and I am his." No earthly partnership compares with the harmony and bliss of this heavenly marriage.

And there will be permanence, for this union will not be vulnerable to misunderstandings, bitterness, and alienation. It will be the perfect match, and subsequent life will only deepen the relationship—forever.

In the Rapture, Jesus will catch us up; at the judgment seat He will clean us up; and at the Marriage Supper He will cheer us up! Then will follow a thousand-year honeymoon during Jesus' millennial rule.

> For in the resurrection they neither marry nor are given in marriage, but are like angels in heaven.
> —MATTHEW 22:30

Worldly marriages in which we are bound to be faithful to one husband or wife will cease as Christ comes and takes us to be with Him. Once we get to heaven, there will be no marital relationship between us and the one with whom we were married here on Earth.

WAR IN HEAVEN

There will be a war between God's angels and the devil and his angels. After their defeat, the devil and his angels will be thrown down to the earth. (See Revelation 12:7–12.)

The scripture states that Lucifer, an "angel of God who was in authority in the presence of God," rebelled against God.

> But you said in your heart, "I will ascend
> to heaven; I will raise my throne above the
> stars of God, And I will sit on the mount of
> assembly in the recesses of the north. I will
> ascend above the heights of the clouds; I will
> make myself like the Most High."
>
> —Isaiah 14:13–14

Lucifer and his followers made open warfare against the Father, the Son, the Holy Ghost, and the eternal plan of salvation and were cast down to earth. (See Isaiah 14:15; Jude 1:6).

After the Marriage Supper of the Lord, there will be a war in heaven that will not be seen with the naked eye by the people still left on the earth as the seven-year Tribulation starts to unfold.

There Are Three Places That Are Called Heaven in the Bible

1) Atmospheric heaven

The expansion that surrounds the Earth, which our naked eyes can see, is the very first "heaven" that comes to our imagination. This contains our atmosphere—the oxygen that we breathe and other gases that support our existence. This in turn controls our seasons, stores our water supply, and determines our weather. We might refer to it as the *atmospheric heaven*.

2) The celestial heaven

The second heaven is a much broader belt of space. It contains the heavenly bodies, such as the sun, moon, and stars. This is the celestial heaven, which is remote from the Earth's atmospheric heaven. This, of course, is taking into consideration our normal life span, the number of light years we are away from most of the planets, and the speed at which we can travel in space. A rocket travelling through space at twenty-five thousand miles per hour would have to travel 114,367 years to reach the nearest star, so huge and vast is the celestial heaven.

3) The abode of God

Astronomical discoveries prove that beyond the second heaven there is a vast and immeasurable empty space. This may be the third heaven that is mentioned in the Bible as the abode of God.

> Look down from heaven and see from Your holy and glorious habitation.
> —Isaiah 63:15

> And you were dead in your trespasses and sins, in which you formerly walked according to the course of this world, according to the prince of the power of the air, of the spirit that is now working in the sons of disobedience.
> —Ephesians 2:1–2

Satan obviously knows his time is short and he is becoming very furious. In the End Times, Satan will have the last three and one-half years of the Tribulation to create as much havoc as he can through the Antichrist and false prophet before Jesus comes back and finally puts an end to his reign of terror.

And there was war in heaven, Michael and his angels waging war with the dragon. The dragon and his angels waged war, and they were not strong enough, and there was no longer a place found for them in heaven. And the great dragon was thrown down, the serpent of old who is called the devil and Satan, who deceives the whole world; he was thrown down to the earth, and his angels were thrown down with him. Then I heard a loud voice in heaven, saying, "Now the salvation, and the power, and the kingdom of our God and the authority of His Christ have come, for the accuser of our brethren has been thrown down, he who accuses them before our God day and night. And they overcame him because of the blood of the Lamb and because of the word of their testimony, and they did not love their life even when faced with death. For this reason, rejoice, O heavens and you who dwell in them. Woe to the earth and the sea, because the devil has come down to you, having great wrath, knowing that he has only a short time. And when the dragon saw that he was thrown down to the earth, he persecuted the woman who gave birth to the male child. But the two wings of the great eagle were given to the woman, so that she could fly into the wilderness to her place, where she was nourished for a time and times and half a time, from the presence of the serpent. And the serpent poured water like a river out of his mouth after the woman, so that he might cause her to be swept away with the flood. But the earth helped the woman, and the earth opened its mouth and drank up the river which the dragon poured out of his mouth. So the dragon was enraged with the woman, and went off to make war with the rest of her children, who keep the commandments of God and hold to the testimony of Jesus.

—Revelation 12:7–17

Let the information we have received in the above bring transformation within us and prepare us to meet the Lord. Amen.

TO CONTACT THE AUTHOR

chandrapublishing@yahoo.ca